QL 676.5 B7 1974   74-603

Brann,
How to build birdhouses
and a bird feeder.

Date Due

JUL 2000

JUN 2004

JAN 09

JUL X X 2015

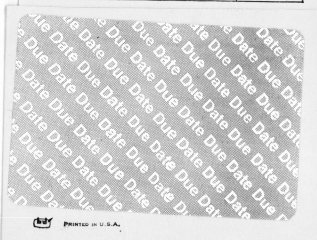

HOW TO BUILD

Birdhouses
and
Bird Feeders

by donald r.brann

Library of Congress Card No. 67-14311

REVISED EDITION – 1974

Published by:

DIRECTIONS SIMPLIFIED, INC.

Division of

EASI-BILD PATTERN CO., INC.

Briarcliff Manor, N.Y.

Page 43

Page 62

Page 31

Page 54

Page 24

Page 37

Page 6

Page 47

5

HOW TO BUILD A MARTIN HOUSE

Step-by-step directions explain how to build a 16 apartment martin house, two bird feeders, three wren houses and a bluebird house.

A martin house is an interesting project because martins are fascinating birds. They are probably the cleanest and most clannish of all. They always seek out their own kind, like living in apartment-style houses because they enjoy each other's company, and, odd as it may seem, martins really like people better than most birds. In fact, martins like people better than people like people.

The old maxim "Birds of a feather flock together" was probably conceived by someone studying the social life of a martin.

Watch bird behavior and you will be amazed to see how nature practices desegregation through co-existence. First you will see a group of sparrows bathing in a puddle. After they have gone, the red-breasted robins will march across a lawn looking for worms. These will be followed by blue jays, those beautiful, but pesky scavengers, and so it goes. Most birds live, and let live, and seldom fight other birds.

According to agricultural bulletins, a purple martin is a great bird to have around since they eat almost 2000 mosquitoes a day. Punctual in their habits, martins invariably return to the same house, the same time each year, and always go back to the apartment they previously occupied.

Being friendly birds, martins don't particularly mind a lawn mower, household chores or other distractions. They learn to live with people and like it.

Read step-by-step directions through completely before buying materials. Note location of each part in each illustration when same is mentioned. To compensate for any variation in lumber width or thickness, always measure inner framing members against actual construction before cutting. Apply waterproof glue to all parts before nailing together.

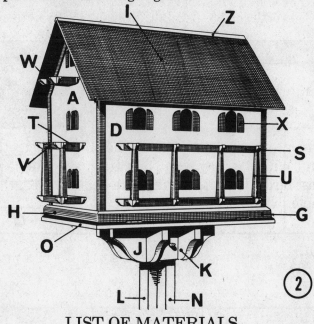

LIST OF MATERIALS

1—¼"x4'x8' exterior grade plywood for A, D, I, P, Q, R, X, Y, and Z.

1—5/4x6"x6' for J, K.

1—2x4x16' for L — length optional

2—1x2x16' for N — buy same length as L

3—1x2x12' for B, C, E, F, G, H, S, T, U, V, and W.

1—¾"x2'x3' Ext. grade plywood for M, O.

In drawing up step-by-step directions we figured a 1x2 as measuring ¾"x1½"; 2x4 - 1½"x3½"; 5/4x6"- 1⅛"x5 ½".

1—Box 1" No. 16 Wire Brads

1—Box 1¼" No. 16 Wire Brads

½ lb. 6 Penny Finishing Nails

20—1¼" No. 8 Flathead Wood Screws

8—1¾" No. 10 Flathead Wood Screws

2—3½" Butt Hinges

2—1" Hooks and Eyes

Use ¼″ Ext. grade plywood for ends A, sides D, roof I, ridge — trim Y and Z, shutters, apartment walls Q, R, Illus. 3.

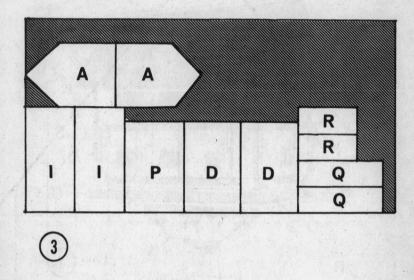

③

Cut 1x2 to ¾″x¾″ for B, C, F.

Cut two ends A — 15½″x23″, Illus. 4. Note cutting chart.

Draw a line through center of A from ridge to floor. Using a two foot square, draw lines to indicate angle of roof, position of entry holes, perch V and W, etc.

Drill 1¾″ holes in position indicated.

Many martin experts recommend a 1¾″ or 2″ opening, others prefer shape shown in Illus. 5. Using a sabre or keyhole saw, cut openings to shape of full size pattern, Illus. 5. Sandpaper each opening. Fill any openings in edge with a wood filler. When dry, sandpaper smooth.

Cut two sides D — 15¼″x22⅝″, Illus. 6. Follow same procedure to locate and drill holes for other openings. If you don't have an expansion bit, drill a hole, insert a keyhole saw to cut openings. A good sabre saw will cut openings without pre-drilling.

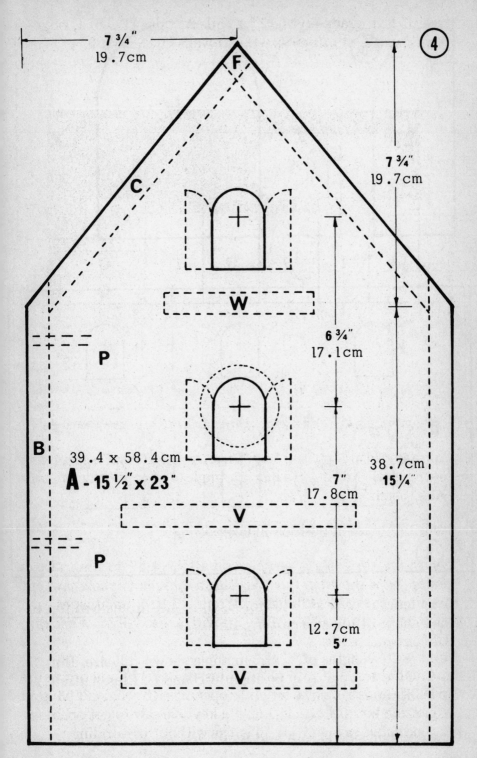

7 ¾"
19.7cm

4

F

7 ¾"
19.7cm

C

+

W

6 ¾"
17.1cm

P

B

39.4 x 58.4 cm

A - 15 ½" x 23"

+

38.7cm
15 ¼"

7"
17.8cm

V

P

+

12.7cm
5"

V

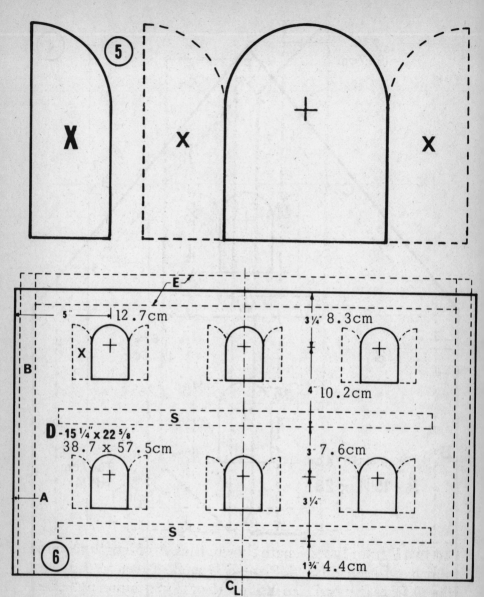

Cut 4 lengths of ¾″x¾″x16″ for B, Illus. 4. Cut angle at top to exact shape of full-size pattern, Illus. 7.

Cut 4 − 10″ lengths of ¾″x¾″ to angle shown full-size, Illus. 7 for C. Glue and nail A in position to B and C, Illus. 4, using 1″ No. 16 Brads.

Glue and nail side D to A and B.

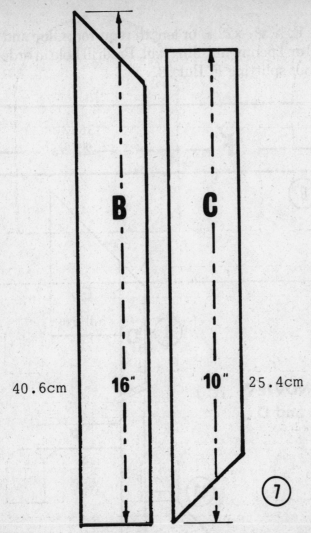

B

C

40.6cm   **16"**   **10"**   25.4cm

⑦

Cut two E from 1x2 to length shown, Illus. 8, or length required to fit in position, Illus. 6. Plant E D angle shown in end view, Illus. 9. Glue and nail E to inside face of D in position indicated, Illus. 6.

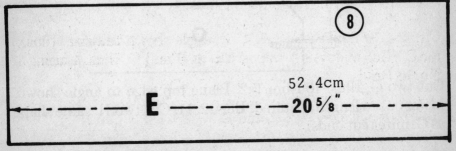

⑧

52.4cm

E ———— · **20 ⁵⁄₈"** · ——

Cut ridge F. ¾"x¾"x22⅛" or length required. Glue and nail F to C with a 3 or 4 penny finishing nail. Predrill hole in order to drive nail without splitting F, Illus. 8.

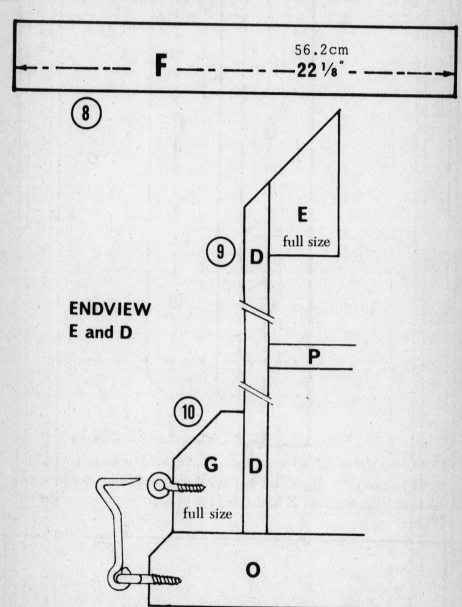

F — 56.2cm — 22 ⅛"

ENDVIEW
E and D

E full size

D

P

G full size

D

O

Cut two G, Illus. 10 from 1x2. Plane top edge to angle shown. Miter cut to length required, Illus. 2, 11. Cut two H, same shape as G, miter cut ends.

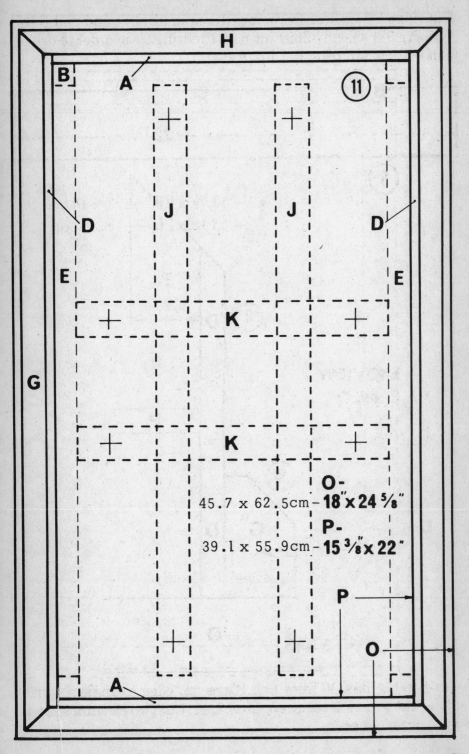

H

B

A

⑪

J

J

D

D

E

E

+

K

+

G

+

K

+

O-
45.7 x 62.5cm - **18"x 24 ⅝"**

P-
39.1 x 55.9cm - **15 ⅜" x 22"**

P

O

A

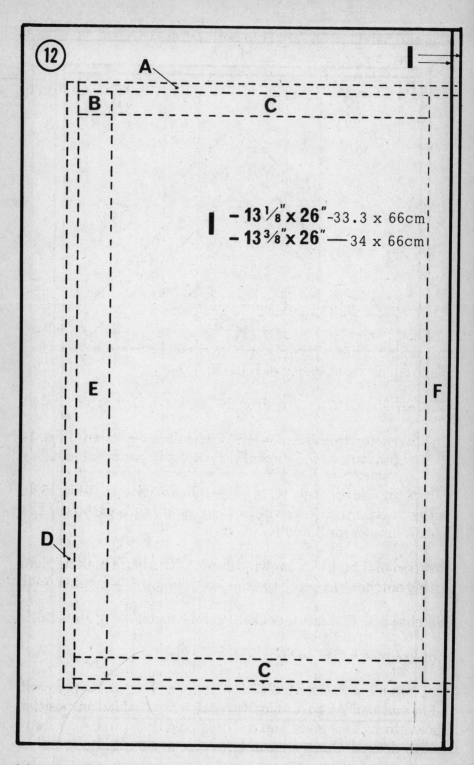

⑫

A

B

C

I — **13 ⅛″ × 26″** -33.3 x 66cm
— **13 ⅜″ × 26″** — 34 x 66cm

E

F

D

C

Glue and nail D to G, A to H in position shown, Illus. 11. G and H act as a water table to shed water.

Cut roof I. Cut one 13⅛"x26", one 13⅜"x26", Illus. 12. Glue and nail roof together in position shown, Illus. 13.

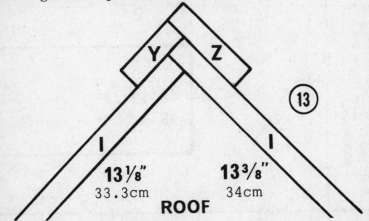

ROOF

Cut floor O, Illus. 11, 18"x24⅝" from ¾" Ext. grade plywood. Plane edge to shape shown, Illus. 10.

Cut two floors, P, 15⅜"x22" from ¼" plywood. Do not bevel edge.

Cut two house brackets J — 20". Use full-size pattern, Illus. 14 to cut both ends shape shown. Cut angles in position indicated.

Cut two house brackets K, 14". Use full-size pattern, Illus. 15, to cut both ends shape shown. Cut angles in position shown. Use 5/4x6" lumber for J and K.

Position of J and K is shown, Illus. 11. To insure making tight fitting notches, cut notch to exact thickness of 5/4" lumber used.

Notches in J K create a pocket to receive pole L M, Illus. 16.

Cut 2x4 pole L, 3¼" wide.

Cut two filler blocks M, 3⅛"x3⅛" from ¾" Ext. grade plywood. Glue and nail M to L. Cut two 1x2's for N. Nail in position shown to L. This gives you a strong pole that can be built any length desired. Plane edge of L if necessary to fit into J K.

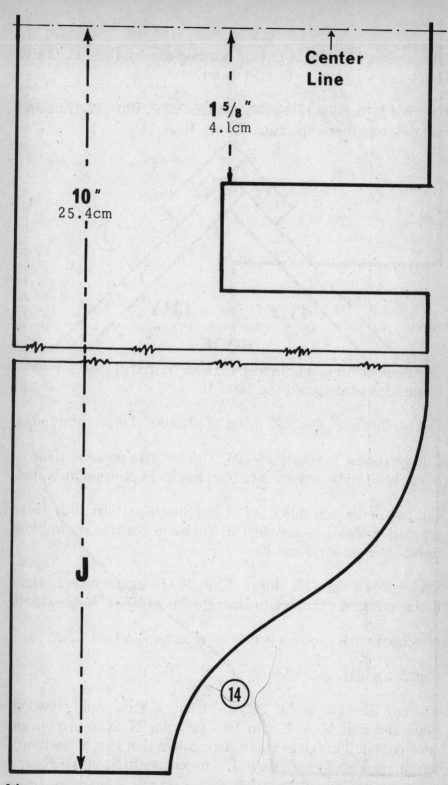

Center
Line

1 ⅝"
4.1cm

10"
25.4cm

J

⑭

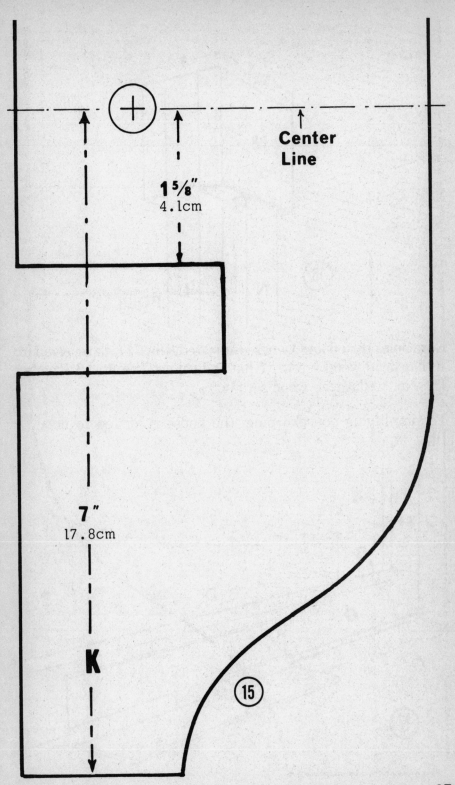

**Center
Line**

1⅝"
4.1cm

7"
17.8cm

K

⑮

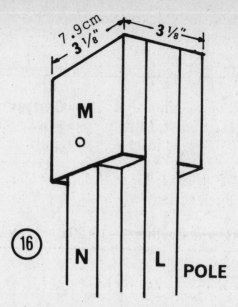

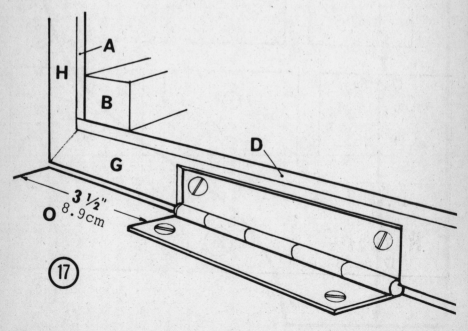

Bore holes thru floor O where indicated, Illus. 11, to receive No. 10 flat head wood screws. Glue and screw O to J and K using 1¾" No. 10 flathead wood screws.

To simplifying housekeeping, the house is hinged to floor O, Illus. 17.

Notch G to receive full thickness of hinge. Screw hinge to G and to floor, 3½″ from ends.

Fasten other side to O with 1″ hooks and eyes, Illus. 10.

Place L M end of pole into J K. Plane L if necessary. Drill ½″ hole thru K, M, L and K, Illus. 15. House is locked to pole with an 8″ length of ½″ dowel inserted through K, L and M.

Cut two floors P, Illus. 4, 11, to fit loosely inside of house. Use ¼″ plywood. Notch corners where required to receive B.

Cut partitions Q and R, Illus. 18, 19, 20 to fit freely within house.

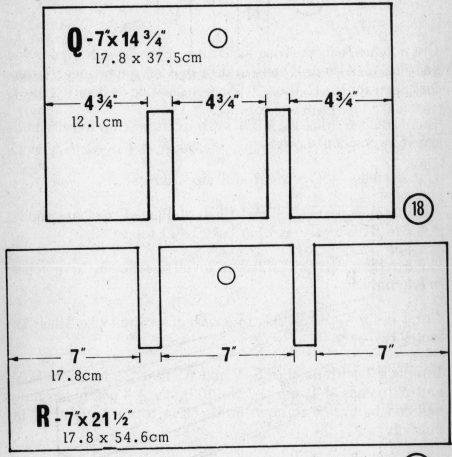

Q - 7″ x 14 ¾″
17.8 x 37.5cm

4 ¾″
12.1cm

4 ¾″

4 ¾″

18

7″
17.8cm

7″

7″

R - 7″ x 21 ½″
17.8 x 54.6cm

19

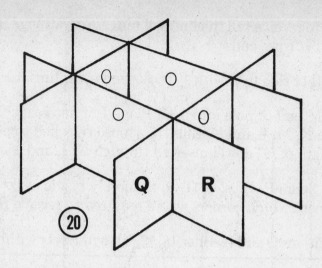

Cut notches to insure snug fit. Drill ½″ holes in Q, R, to provide ventilation. Also drill holes in floor of center apartment. Interlock partitions Q, R, Illus. 20. Place in position on floor P, Illus. 4.

Cut 8 trellis S, Illus. 21, ⅜″x¾″x18¼″. Cut notches full size indicated in position shown.

Cut 28 trellis — T, ⅜″x¾″ to full size, Illus. 21.

Cut 12 trellis posts U, ¾″x¾″, Illus. 22. Plane U to shape shown full size. This measures ¾″ at base, ⅜″ at top.

Cut 8 trellis — V, ⅜″x¾″, Illus. 21, to full size shown. Cut notches in four only.

Cut 4 trellis — W, ⅜″x¾″, to length shown full size, Illus. 21. Notch two only.

Interlock T with notched S, V and W, Illus. 23. Nail rear S, V and W to ends of T, use 1¼″ No. 16 brads. A 4 penny finishing nail can be driven through intersection to anchor post U in position.

A small brad, toe-nailed at bottom of U, will keep post from turning.

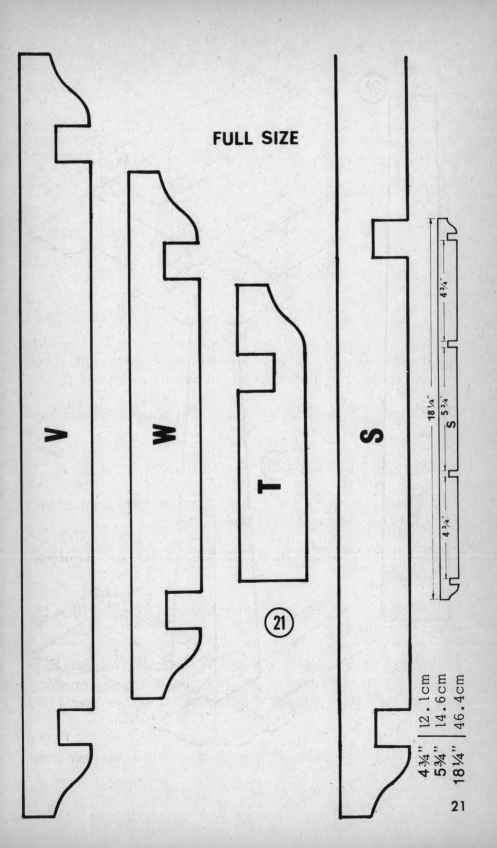

FULL SIZE

V

W

T

S

㉑

18¼"
5¾"
4¾"

4¾"   12.1cm
5¾"   14.6cm
18¼"   46.4cm

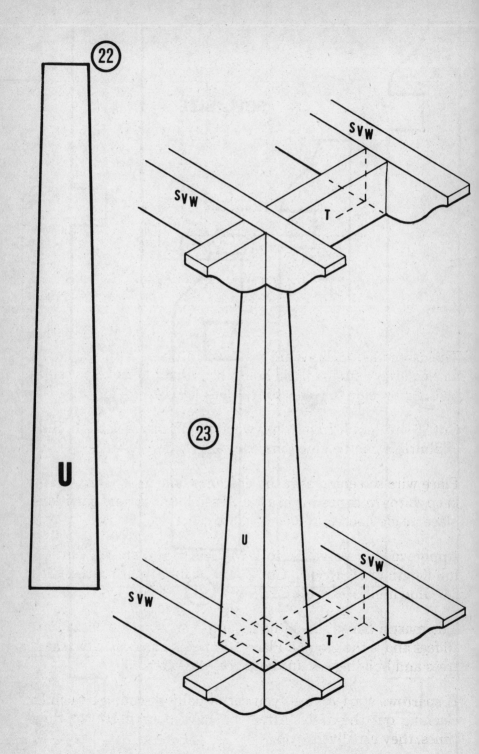

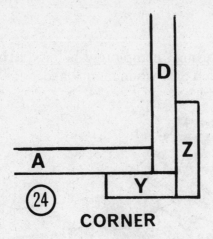

CORNER

The assembled trellises are fastened to house with 1¼" No. 6 flathead wood screws. Drill holes thru A and D and into center of T. Screw side to trellis so it drives into end of T.

Cut 36 shutters X from ¼" plywood to full size of pattern, Illus. 5. Shutters can be glued in position or painted.

Place wire screening over top entrance hole in A, Illus. 4. This keeps birds from nesting in attic. Assemble floors and partitions, place inside house.

Apply wood preservative to L M, Cut trim Z and Y, Illus. 13, full length of I for ridge. Cut Z and Y, for corner boards, Illus. 24. Glue in position, Illus. 2.

The martin house should be mounted on a pole at least 15 to 20 feet above the ground. Place it in the open, away from shade trees and buildings. Paint house color desired.

If sparrows start to nest, you can usually discourage them by cleaning out the nests. After you have done it two or three times, they usually give up.

HOW TO BUILD A BIRD FEEDER

Read directions through completely before cutting any parts. Note location of each part when mentioned. Glue all permanent wood-to-wood parts.

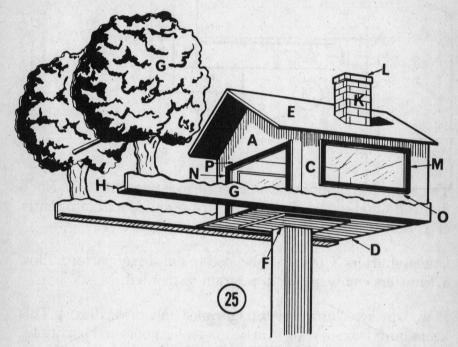

LIST OF MATERIALS

Use ¼″ Ext. grade plywood for all parts except perch.

Cut front A — 6½″ x 10″, to shape shown, Illus. 26. Cut opening 3⅜″ x 6″.

Cut back B, 6½″ x 10″, Illus. 27. Cut opening for window 1¾″ x 6″ in position shown.

Cut two sides C, 4″ x 7″, Illus. 28. Cut opening for window 1¾″ x 4½″ in position shown.

Cut floor D, 9″ x 10½″, Illus. 29.

24

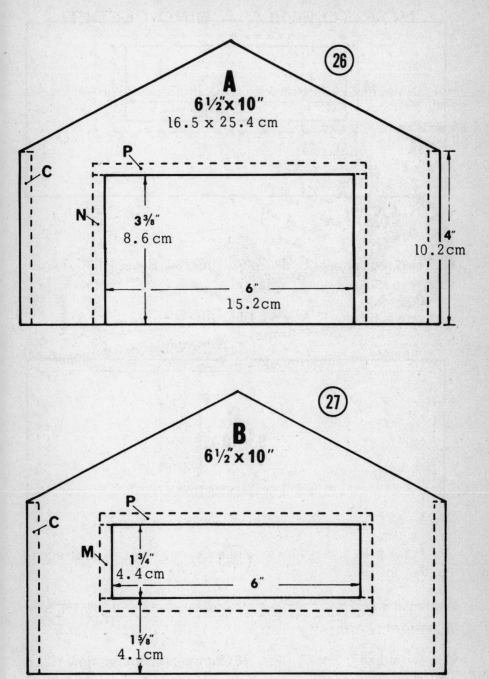

A
6½" x 10"
16.5 x 25.4 cm

C

P

N

3⅜"
8.6 cm

6"
15.2 cm

4"
10.2 cm

㉖

B
6½" x 10"

C

P

M

1¾"
4.4 cm

6"

1⅝"
4.1 cm

㉗

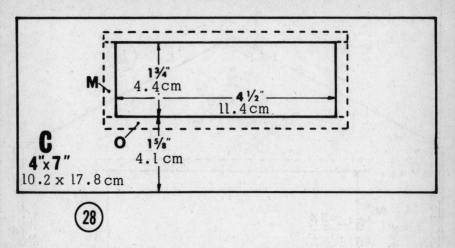

M

1¾"
4.4 cm

4½"
11.4 cm

C
4"x 7"
10.2 x 17.8 cm

O   1⅝"
4.1 cm

(28)

Cut two roof panels E, 6½" x 9", Illus. 30. Bevel edge to angle shown to make a neat fitting ridge.

Cut one sub-base F, 5" x 5", Illus. 31.

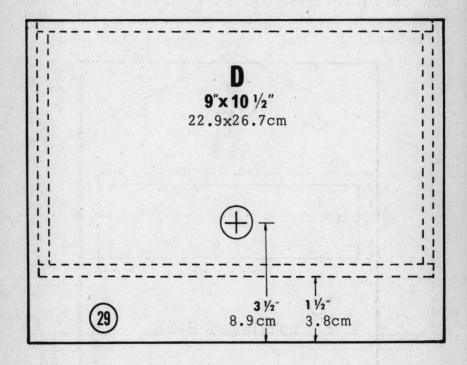

D
9"x 10 ½"
22.9x26.7cm

(29)

3½"
8.9cm

1½"
3.8cm

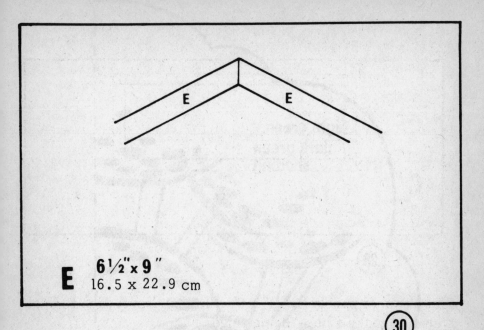

E **6½" x 9"**
16.5 x 22.9 cm

(30)

Cut two vanes G, to full size of pattern. Illus. 32 shows one half. Cut pattern along solid outside lines, trace on plywood, turn over and trace other half. Then draw bottom of G — 1⅛" x 15" as shown, Illus. 33, 25. Drill ½" hole in position noted.

(31)

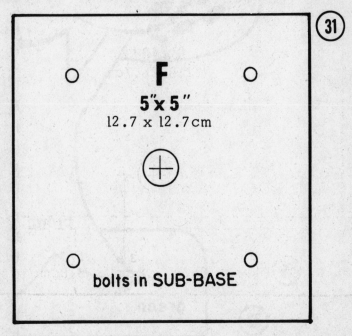

F
5" x 5"
12.7 x 12.7 cm

bolts in SUB-BASE

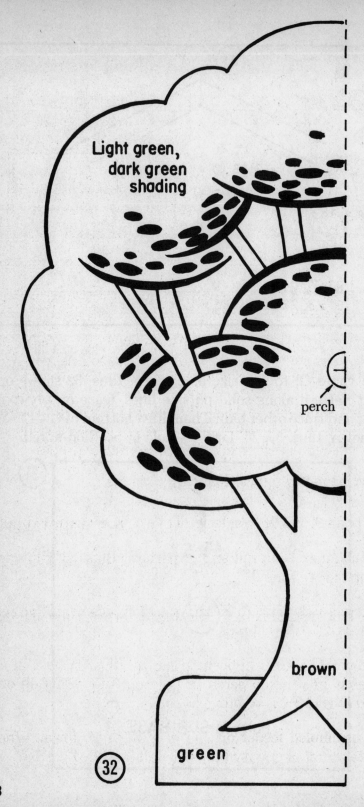

Light green,
dark green
shading

perch

brown

green

(32)

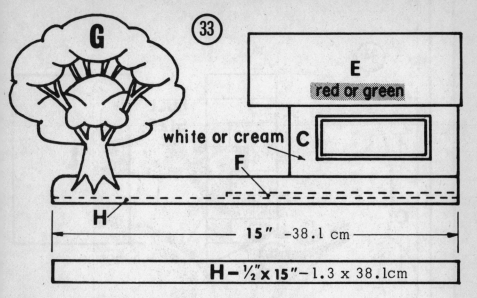

Cut two stiffeners H, ½" x 15", Illus. 33, 25.

Glue and nail G to H.

Cut window frames M, N, O, P, Illus. 34 to full size of patterns. Note position of each, Illus. 26, 27, 28. Cut clear plastic for windows. Fasten plastic in position with window frames.

These can be nailed in position with ½" brads.

Glue and nail A and B to sides C; D to A, B, C, with 1" brads.

Cut one chimney K to full size of pattern, Illus. 35. Chimney K and top L are optional.

Glue and nail L to K; E to K with four 1" brads. Glue and nail roof to A, B, C, with 1" brads.

Glue and nail G H to D in position shown, Illus. 25, 33. Cut ½" dowel perch 10½". Glue perch in position, Illus. 32. Bolt sub base F to D with ¼" x ¾" stove bolts.

Balance assembled feeder on end of a ¾" or 1" dowel. When you locate center of gravity bore hole in F and D, Illus. 36.

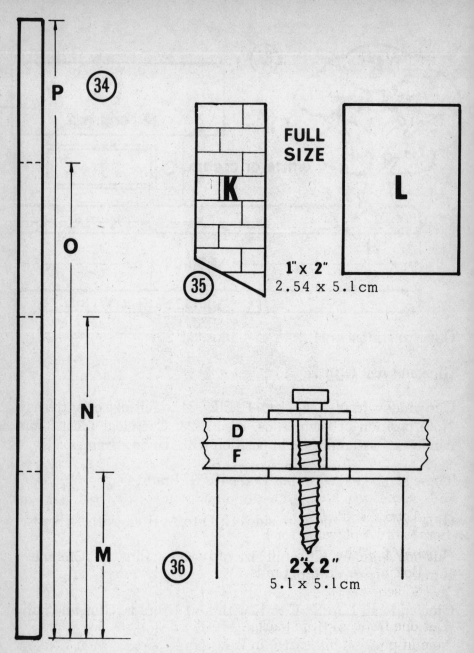

FULL SIZE

K

1" x 2"
2.54 x 5.1 cm

L

D
F

2"x 2"
5.1 x 5.1 cm

Before mounting feeder on a pole, sandpaper all edges and surfaces smooth, paint colors suggested, Illus. 32, 33.

Mount feeder on a 2x2x6′ or higher pole with a ¼″ x 2″ lag screw. Do not tighten lag screw. Allow base to move freely as weather vane.

HOW TO BUILD A BLUEBIRD HOUSE

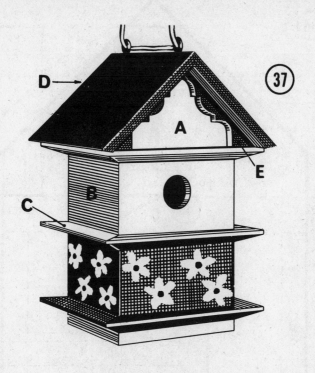

LIST OF MATERIALS

1 — ½″ x 2′ x 3′ Ext. grade plywood for A, B, D, E, G
1 — 1 x 6 x 4′ for C
Scraps of ¼″ plywood for F
4 penny finishing nails
1 — Box ¾″ No. 15 wire brads
2 — ⅜″ screw eyes

Cut one front and one back A — 6½″ x 14″, Illus. 38. Bore 1½″ hole in position indicated, in front only. Bore ⅜″ vent hole, in position indicated, in front and back.

Cut two sides B, 5½″ x 11⅛″, Illus. 39. Bevel top edge of B to angle shown, Illus. 38, 39.

Glue and nail A to B with 4 penny finishing nails.

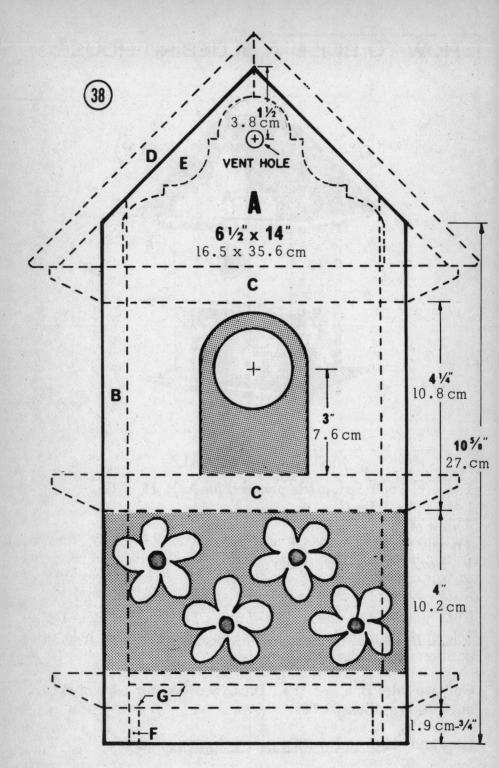

38

1½"
3.8 cm

VENT HOLE

D   E

A

6½" x 14"
16.5 x 35.6 cm

C

B

3"
7.6 cm

4¼"
10.8 cm

C

10⅝"
27. cm

4"
10.2 cm

G

F

1.9 cm-¾"

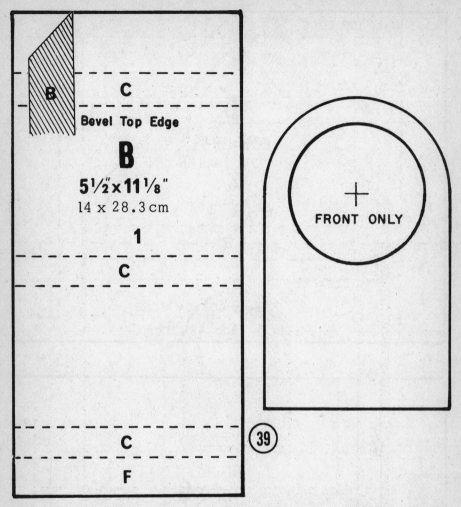

B

B

5½″ x 11⅛″

14 x 28.3 cm

Bevel Top Edge

C

C

C

F

FRONT ONLY

⒊⒐

Cut 12 cornice C, to length and width shown, Illus. 40. Note position of C, Illus. 38. Check length of each piece, then miter cut to exact size required. Apply glue and nail C in position with two 4 penny finishing nails. Drive nails from inside house.

④⓪

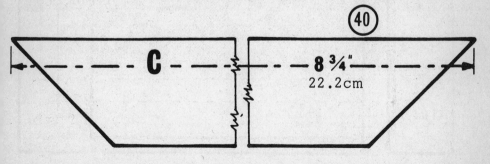

C

8 ¾″

22.2cm

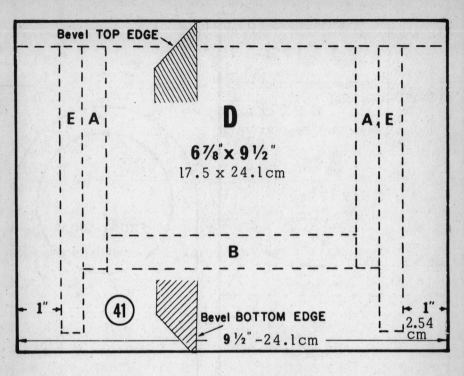

Bevel TOP EDGE

E A

D

6⅞" x 9½"

17.5 x 24.1cm

A E

B

1"

④① 41

Bevel BOTTOM EDGE

9½"-24.1cm

1"
2.54
cm

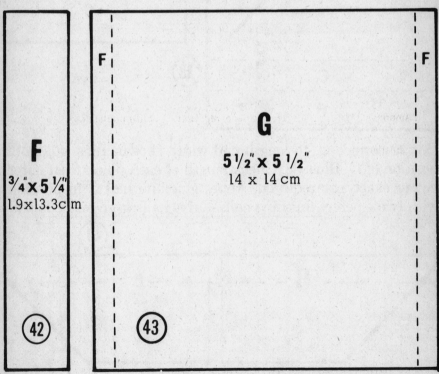

F

¾" x 5¼"

1.9x13.3cm

F

G

5½" x 5½"

14 x 14 cm

F

④② 42

④③ 43

Cut two roof D, 6⅞" x 9½", Illus. 41. Bevel top and bottom edge to angle shown full size.

Glue and nail D to A B with 4 penny finishing nails.

Cut 4 rafters E to full size shown, Illus. 44. Glue and nail in position to A with ¾" No. 15 brads, Illus. 38.

Cut 2 cleats F — ¼" x ¾" x 5½", Illus. 42. Glue and nail F to inside face of B, in position shown, Illus. 39.

Cut 1 floor G — ½" x 5½" x 5½", Illus. 43, G rests on cleats F. Do not glue or nail. This permits cleaning house when necessary.

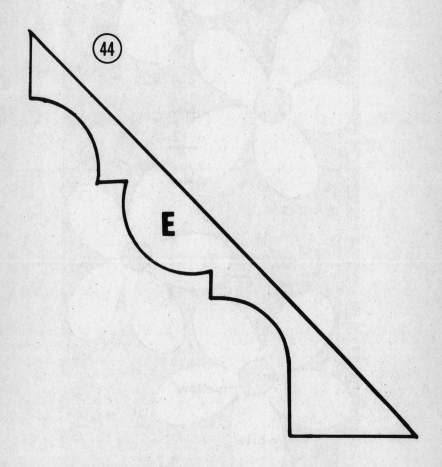

Full size decorating pattern is shown, Illus. 45. Paint design colors suggested.

Fasten two screw eyes in ridge. Hang house from branch in tree.

HOW TO BUILD A WREN HOUSE

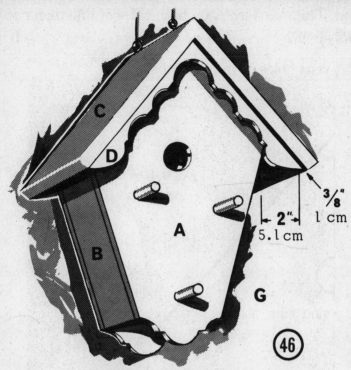

LIST OF MATERIALS

1 — ½″ x 12″ x 48″ Ext. grade plywood for A, B, C, D, F
1 — ⅜″ dowel — 9″ — G
Scraps ¼″ plywood — E
4 penny finishing nails
1 Box ½″ brads
1 Box 1″ brads
2 — ⅜″ screw eyes

Cutting chart, Illus. 47, suggests layout for cutting parts.

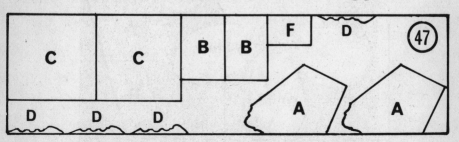

Trace 48 a and 48 aa along solid black outside lines. Tape two parts together where indicated. Draw a straight line on ½″ plywood. Trace pattern A on both sides of line then cut two A to shape shown.

Bore ⅜″ vent holes in front and back.

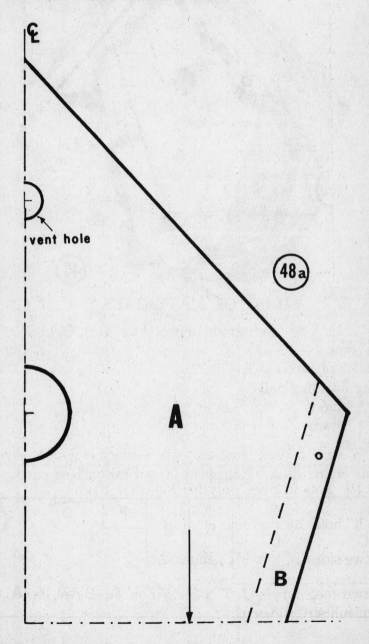

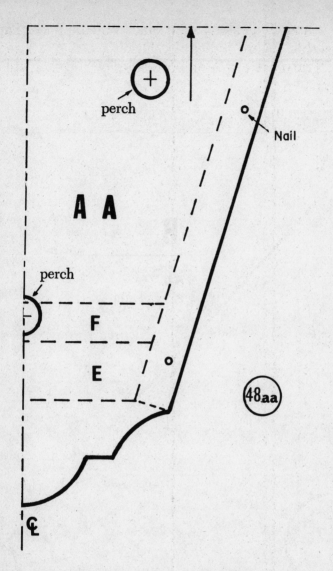

Bore ⅞″ or 1″ hole in front only for Berwick or House Wren.

Bore 1⅛″ hole in front only for Carolina Wren.

Bore ⅜″ holes for perches.

Cut two sides B, 4″ x 6¾″, Illus. 49.

Cut two roof panels C, 7″ x 8¼″, Illus. 50. Bevel top edge as shown full size, Illus. 51.

B

4"x6¾"

10.2 x 17.1 cm

(49)

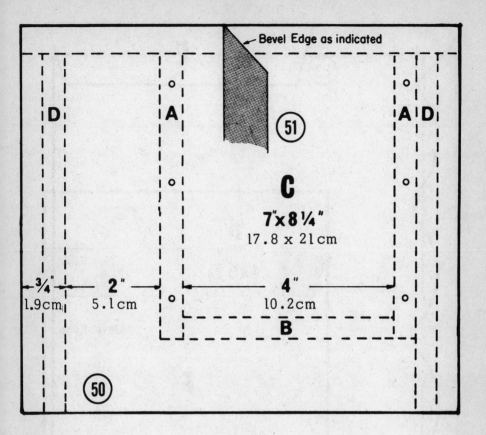

Bevel Edge as indicated

D | A | (51) | A | D

C
7" x 8 ¼"
17.8 x 21 cm

¾"
1.9cm | 2"
5.1cm | 4"
10.2cm

B

(50)

Cut four fascia D, to full size of pattern, Illus. 52.

Cut two cleats E, use ¼" plywood, Illus. 53.

Cut floor F, 3" x 4", Illus. 54. Bevel edge where indicated to angle shown full size.

Glue and nail E in position indicated to inside face of A. Use ½" brads.

Glue and nail A to B with 4 penny finishing nails.

Bevel top edge of B to conform to pitch of roof.

Glue and nail D to C with 1" brads.

Glue and nail C to A with 4 penny finishing nails.

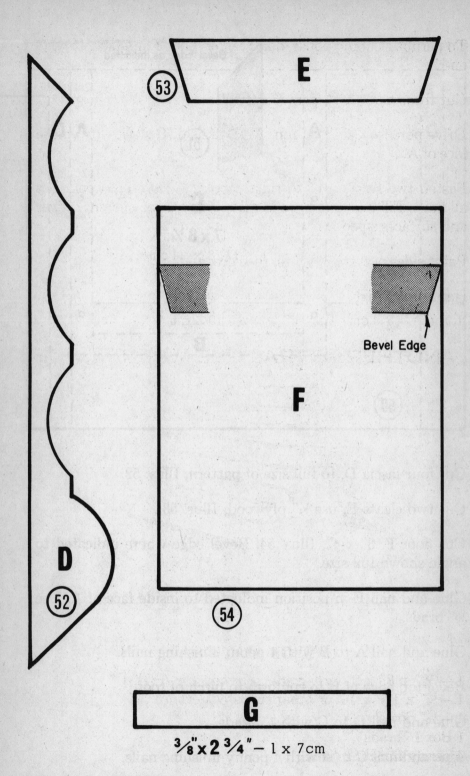

E

㊼

Bevel Edge

F

㊴

D

㊼

G

⅜" x 2¾" − 1 x 7cm

42

To permit cleaning house, don't fasten floor F in place. It rests on E.

Cut three perches G from ⅜" dowel.

Drive perches G in position. Keep ends of G flush with inside face of A.

Fasten two screw eyes to ridge, about 1" from each end. Set all nails. Fill holes with wood filler. Sandpaper opening, edges and surfaces smooth.

Paint sides and front white, roof green.

Hang fairly high.

ANOTHER ATTRACTIVE WREN HOUSE

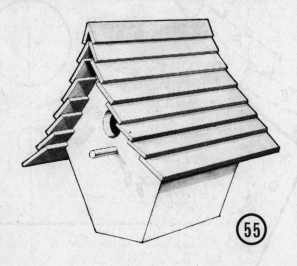

LIST OF MATERIALS

1 — ½" x 8" x 2' Ext. grade plywood for A, B, C
1 — ¼" x 1⅜" x 10' or other size stock lattice
1 — ¼" dowel
1 Box 1" brads
4 penny finishing nails

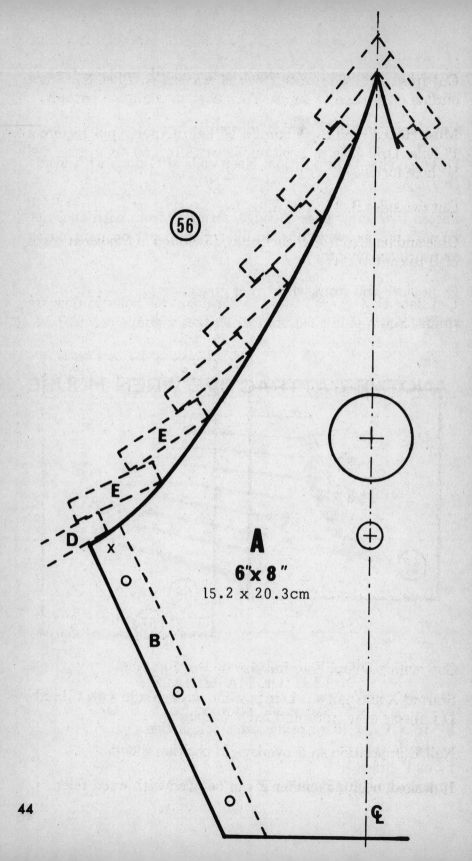

(56)

D
x
E
E
A
6" x 8"
15.2 x 20.3cm
B

C_L

44

Cut front and back to full size of pattern A, Illus. 56. Trace outline on a piece of paper. Turn over to complete pattern.

Most House Wrens can enter a ⅞″ hole. Other types require a 1″ hole. Drill hole in position shown, Illus. 56, in front. Drill ¼″ hole for dowel.

Cut two sides B, 3⅝″ x 4″, Illus. 57.

Glue and nail front and back to B. Plane top and bottom edges of B to conform to A.

Cut floor C, 3″ x 4¾″, Illus. 58. Drill two ¼″ holes in floor for drains. Screw C in position. Plane edges to shape required.

B

3⅝″x 4″

9 x 2 x 10.2 cm

57

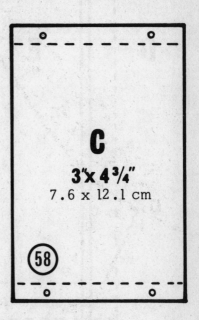

C

3″x 4¾″

7.6 x 12.1 cm

58

Cut roofing D and E to full size shown, Illus. 59.

Start at X and nail one D in position on each side with 1″ brads. D projects over front and back as shown.

Nail E in position so it overlaps in position shown.

If desired, openings under E can be filled with wood filler.

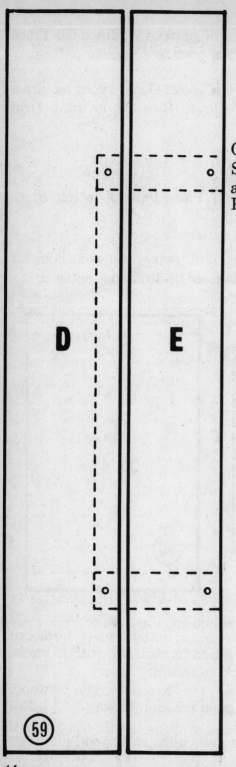

Cut ¼″ dowel, 2″ for a perch.
Sandpaper edge of opening and
all surfaces smooth.
Paint or stain.

D

E

59

LARGE BIRD FEEDER

Illus. 60 shows a large family size feeder that usually attracts a lot of traffic. Since the entire center column contains food that continually replenishes opening at bottom, many birds can be fed before it's necessary to refill.

All parts can be cut from ½″, ⅝″ or ¾″ exterior grade plywood, except back F, roof G, and chimney facing H and K. This can be cut from ¼″ hardboard. Glass or clear plastic can be used in the center column.

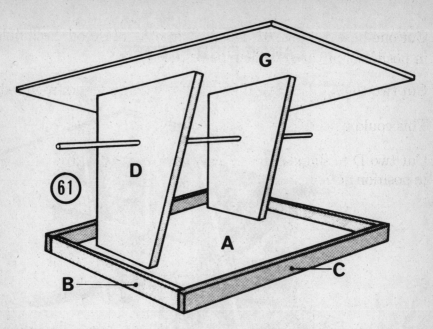

The base A, Illus. 61, 62, provides ample deck space for all guests. While step-by-step illustrations indicate size of each piece, due to variance in lumber thickness always measure and cut parts to exact size your feeder requires after you have begun initial assembly.

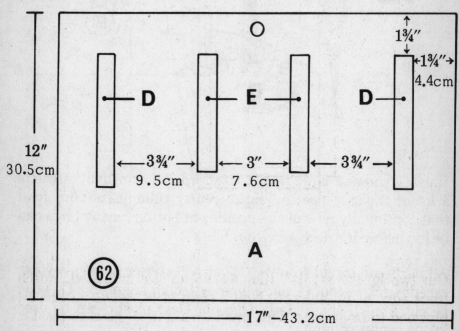

Cut one base A, Illus. 62, 12″ x 17″ from ½″ plywood. Drill hole in position indicated to fit pipe or pole.

Cut two edging B and C, Illus. 61, 1½″ wide by length required.

This could be cut from ⅜″ strips of plywood or lattice.

Cut two D to shape and size shown, Illus. 61, 63. Drill ¼″ hole in position noted.

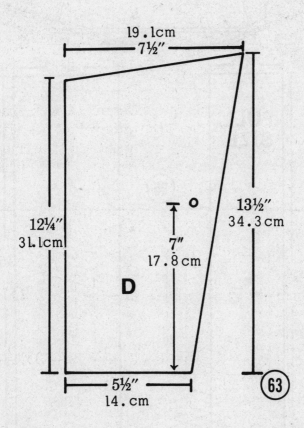

Cut two E, 4½″ x 15¼″, Illus. 64, 65, to size indicated. Notch front edge of E, Illus. 65. Nail a strip of ⅛″ hardboard or ¼″ plywood to front edge. This provides a slot for glass or plastic.

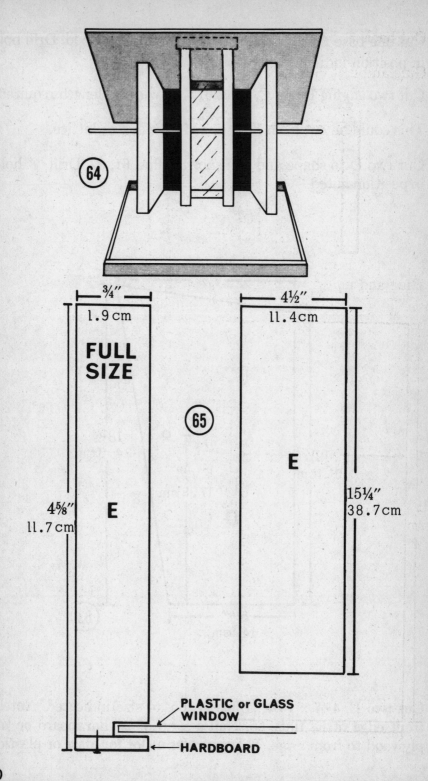

64

65

¾″
1.9 cm

4½″
11.4 cm

FULL SIZE

E

4⅝″
11.7 cm

E

15¼″
38.7 cm

PLASTIC or GLASS WINDOW

HARDBOARD

Cut back F, from ¼″ hardboard, Illus. 66, 12¼″ x 13½″.

Glue and nail F to D & E, Illus. 66, in position shown.

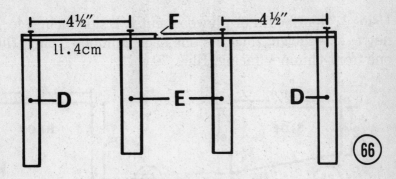

Glue and nail A to D & E in position indicated, Illus. 62.

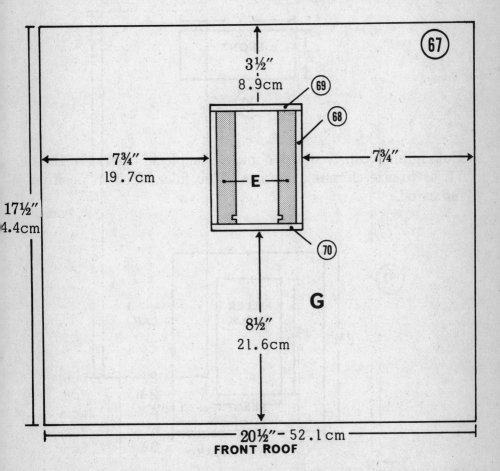

FRONT ROOF

Cut roof G, 17½″ x 20½″ from ¼″ hardboard or plywood, Illus. 67. Cut opening for grain column in position shown. Apply glue and nail G to D and E.

Using ¼″ hardboard or plywood, cut two side facings for chimney to size shown, Illus. 68; one back chimney facing, Illus. 69, one front chimney facing, Illus. 70.

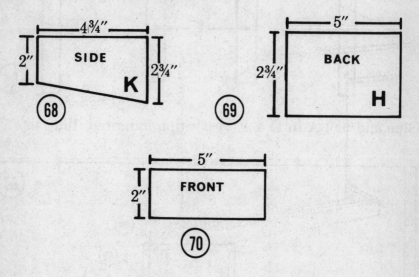

Cut chimney cap, ¾x6¾x6¾″ and a filler block ¾x2¾x4⅝″, Illus. 71, or to size chimney requires. Glue filler block in position indicated.

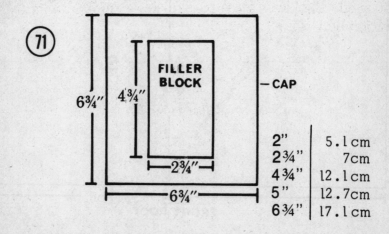

2″	5.1 cm
2¾″	7 cm
4¾″	12.1 cm
5″	12.7 cm
6¾″	17.1 cm

Nail edgings B and C to A, Illus. 61. Cut ¼" dowel 20½" and insert through holes in D. Fasten pipe to feeder with pipe clamps shown. Use ¼" x ⅝" bolts and nuts, Illus. 72.

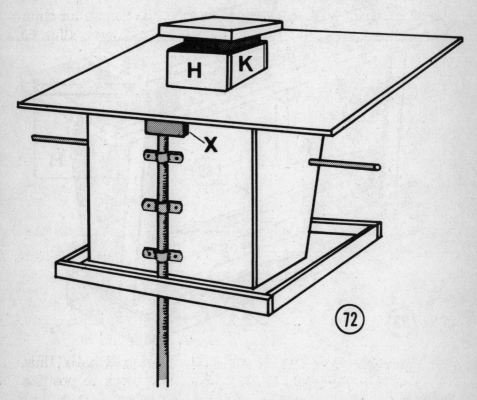

Glue and nail 1"x 2"x 2" pipe stop X, Illus. 72 in position shown.

Cut single thickness glass to size slot requires. Slide glass in position between E, Illus. 64.

AN EASY TO BUILD BIRD FEEDER

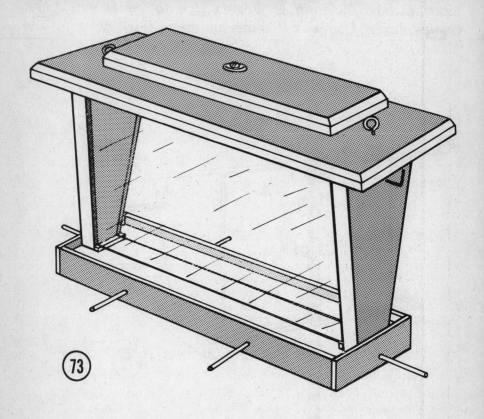

(73)

Regardless of your age, professional background or woodworking talent, a bird feeder, Illus. 73, makes a good starting project.

Cut one A, 3½" x 14" from 1x4, Illus. 74.

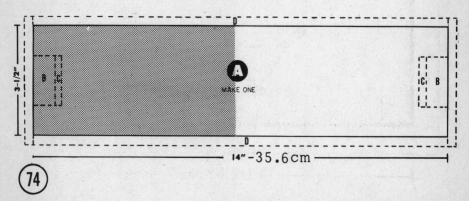

A
MAKE ONE

3-1/2"

14"—35.6cm

(74)

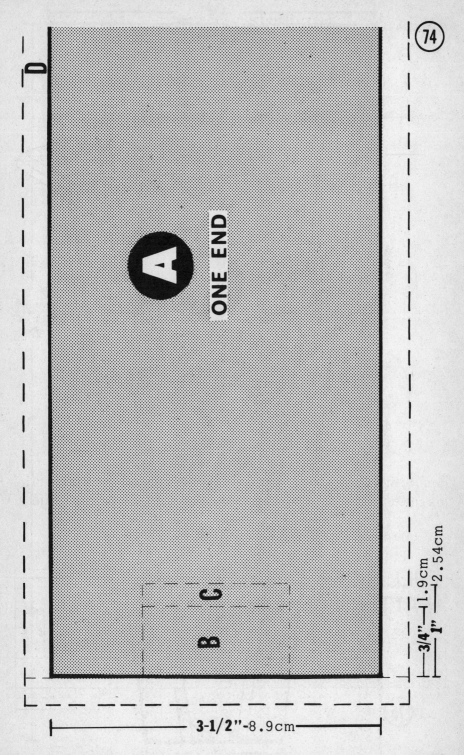

D

A

ONE END

B C

3/4"—1.9cm
1"—2.54cm

3-1/2"-8.9cm

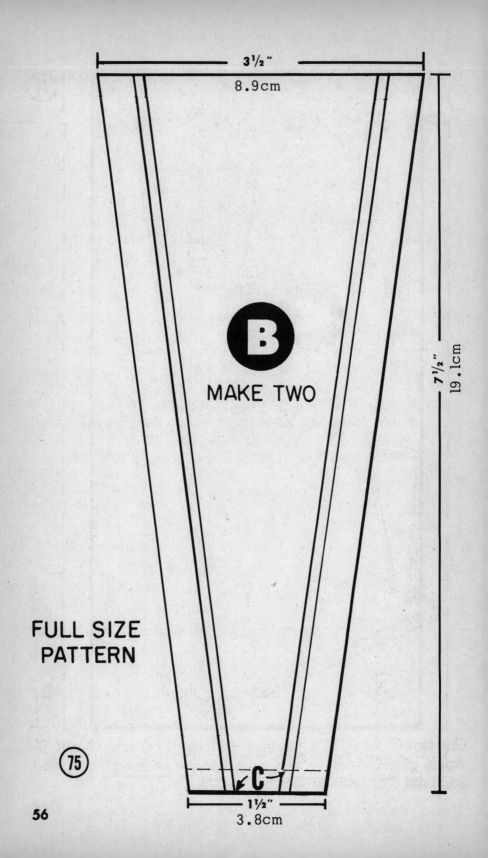

3½"
8.9cm

B

MAKE TWO

7½"
19.1cm

FULL SIZE
PATTERN

C

1½"
3.8cm

75

56

Cut two B, Illus. 75. Cut ⅛″ saw slots, ⅛″ deep, ½″ in from edge.

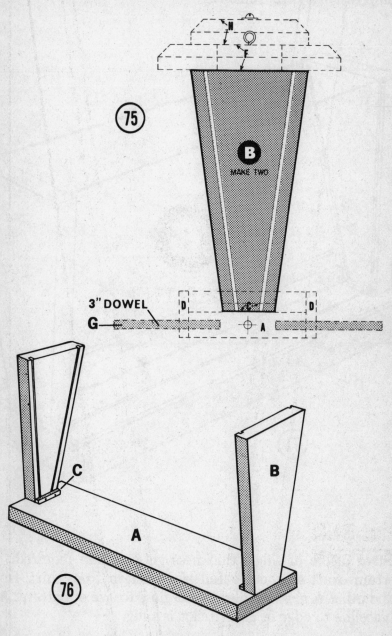

Cut two C, ¼″ x ¼″ x length and shape of bottom edge of B. Apply glue and nail A to B with 6 penny finishing nails. Glue and brad C in position shown, Illus. 76.

Cut two D, ¼″ x 1⅜″ x 4″; two ¼″ x 1⅜″ x 14″. Apply glue. Brad lips in position shown, Illus. 77.

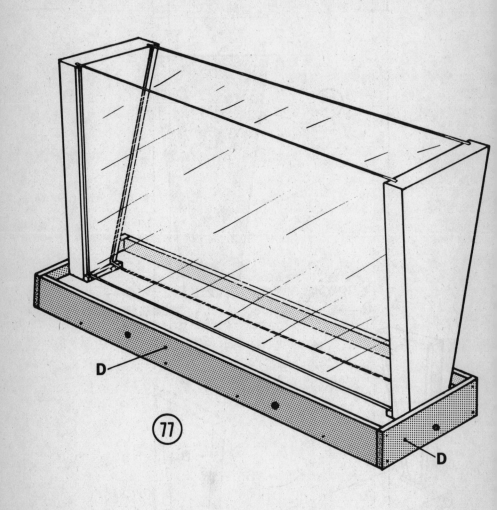

Cut two pieces of single thickness glass to size required. To ascertain exact size, cut a full size pattern from shirt front cardboard. Ask glass retailer to cut glass to size of pattern. Apply vaseline to edge of glass if slot is snug.

Cut F, ¾″ x 5½″ x 14″, Illus. 78. Drill 1¼″ filler holes in position indicated. Using a plane, bevel edge as shown. Carefully nail F to A, Illus. 79.

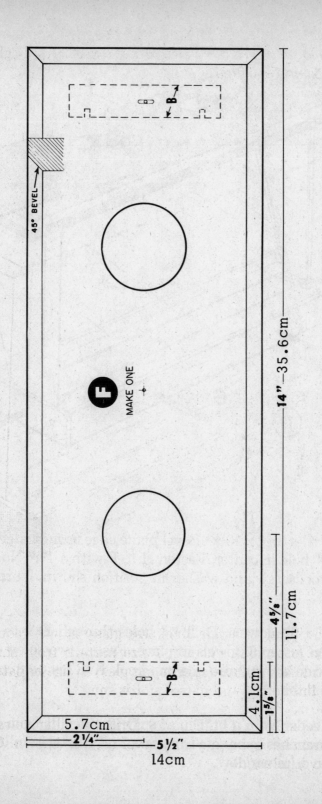

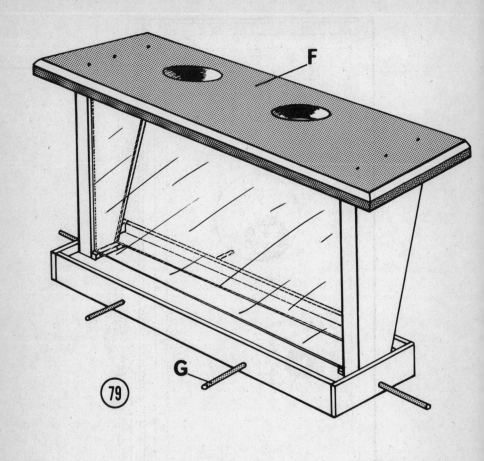

Cut H, ¾″ x 3½″ x 10⅛″. Bevel plane edge as indicated, Illus. 80. Drill ⅛″ hole in center. Fasten H to F with a 1¼″ No. 8 round-head woodscrew and washer in position shown. Turn H to fill feeder.

Cut ¼″ x 3″ dowels. Drill ¼″ holes through D into A. Apply glue and fasten 6 dowels in place. Fasten two screw eyes to F in position shown, also one cup hook K. This permits hanging special tidbits.

Hang feeder from a branch at sufficient height from ground or other branches to be safe from cats, and still be in full view from your favorite window.

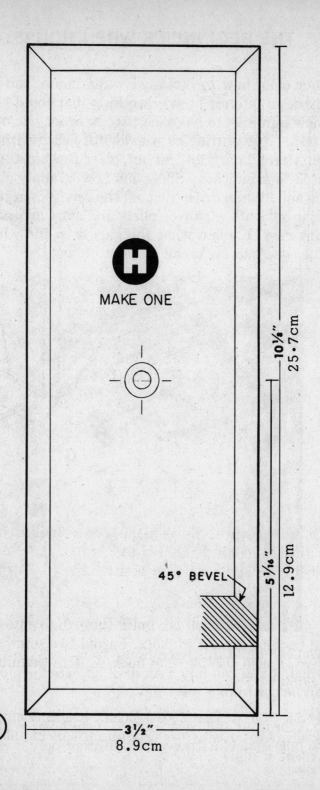

H

MAKE ONE

45° BEVEL

10⅛"
25.7cm

5¹/₁₆"
12.9cm

3½"
8.9cm

80

THE BEGINNER'S WREN HOUSE

Show your child how to build this wren house, and you just might spark an interest in woodworking that could last a lifetime. Show him how to cut each part to exact size of the full size pattern. After cutting to size, identify each with a big A, B, C, etc. After all parts are cut out, place B against A in exact position pattern indicates. Show him how to apply glue. Start the brads and let him drive them all the way. When they bend one, pull it out with a pair of pliers and start another. Make everything easy. Explain what the glue does and why waterproof glue is best to use on all outdoor projects.

While you can build this wren house from 1 x 6, and less than 4′ is needed, if you can buy a scrap of ½″ exterior plywood, all parts can be cut from a piece 12″ x 18″.

Cut two A for front and back. Bore ⅜″ vent holes in both. Bore ⅜″ perch hole and 1″ entrance hole in front only.

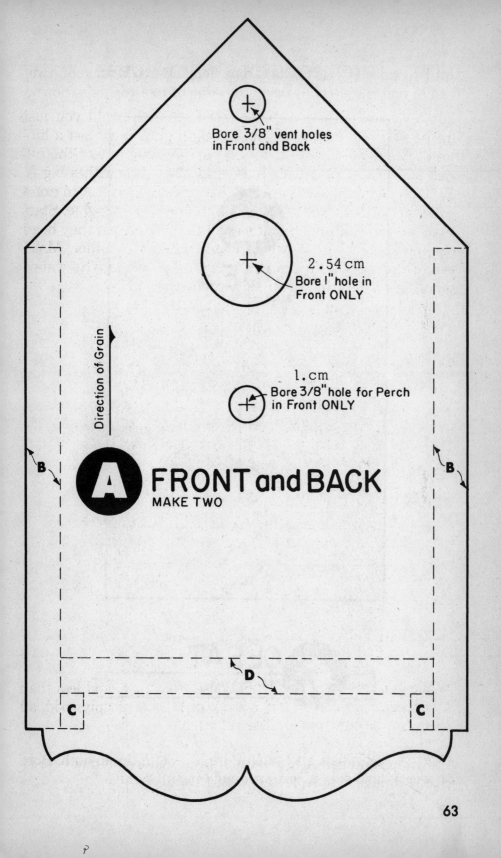

Bore 3/8" vent holes
in Front and Back

2.54 cm
Bore 1" hole in
Front ONLY

Direction of Grain

1 cm
Bore 3/8" hole for Perch
in Front ONLY

A FRONT and BACK
MAKE TWO

B

B

D

C

C

Cut two sides B, two cleats C, one floor D, two E for roof, two trim F, one ⅜″ perch G. Bevel top edge of roof to angle shown.

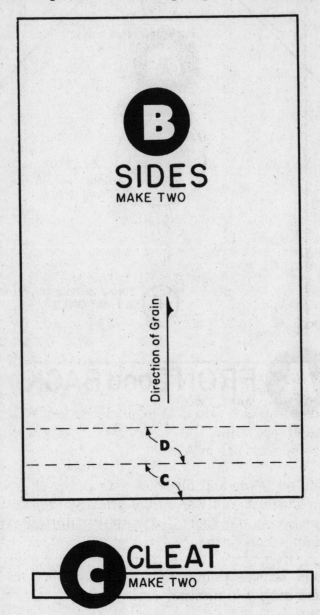

Apply glue and nail A to B with 1″ brads. Glue and nail C to B with ½″ brads, E to A, F to E with 1″ brads.

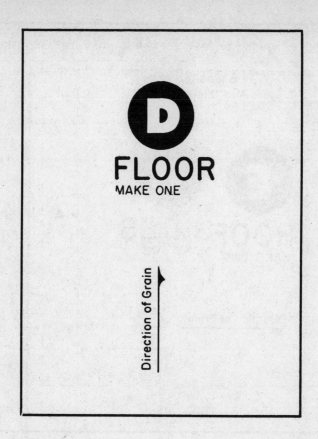

D

FLOOR
MAKE ONE

Direction of Grain

Drive brads through F into E at an angle so they will not protrude through top of roof. Cut ⅜" dowel G to length of pattern, apply glue and insert G in A.

Countersink all brads and fill holes with putty or wood filler made from sawdust and waterproof glue. Sandpaper all surfaces. Paint house and floor. Use exterior paint following the manufacturer's directions.

Screw two ½" screw eyes in roof. Then remove and dip in glue. Fasten them back into position.

To permit cleaning house, the floor isn't nailed. It sets in position on cleats C.

Hang birdhouse.

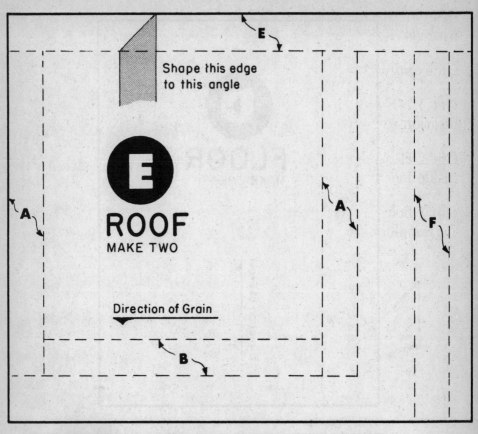

Shape this edge
to this angle

E
ROOF
MAKE TWO

Direction of Grain

F TRIM MAKE TWO

G PERCH MAKE ONE

LIST OF MATERIALS
1 — 1 x 6 x 42″ or
1 — ½″ exterior plywood 12″ x 18″
1 — ⅜″ x 2¾″ dowel
1″ brads
½″ brads
2 — ½″ screweyes
Waterproof glue

7-100